Maria Amata Neyer, O.C.D.

Edith Stein

Her Life in Photos and Documents

About the Author

Maria Amata Neyer, O.C.D., was born in Cologne, Germany, in 1922. She began medical studies, but after her preliminary medical exams she entered the Cologne Carmel in 1944, where she has served numerous terms as prioress since 1961. She established the Edith-Stein-Archiv in the Cologne Carmel and continues to oversee it. She has devoted many years of research to the life of Edith Stein.

Maria Amata Neyer, O.C.D.

Edith Stein
Her Life in Photos and Documents

Translated by Waltraut Stein, Ph.D.

ICS Publications
Institute of Carmelite Studies
2131 Lincoln Road, NE
Washington, DC 20002
1999

EDITH STEIN: HER LIFE IN PHOTOS AND DOCUMENTS is a translation of *Edith Stein: Ihr Leben in Dokumenten und Bildern,* by Maria Amata Neyer (Würzburg, Germany: Echter Verlag, 1987).

Translation authorized. 1987 Echter Verlag Würzburg

ICS Publications
2131 Lincoln Road NE
Washington, DC 20002–1199
800-832-8489

Typeset and produced in the U.S.A.

Library of Congress Cataloging-in-Publication Data

Neyer, Maria Amata, 1922–
  [Edith Stein. English]
  Edith Stein: her life in photos and documents /
Maria Amata Neyer; translated by Waltraut Stein.
     p. cm.
  Includes bibliographical references.
  ISBN 0–935216–66–9 (paper)
  1. Stein, Edith, 1891–1942. 2. Carmelite Nuns—
Germany—Biography. 3. Christian martyrs—Germany—
Biography. 4. Christian philosophers—Germany—
Biography. 5. Stein, Edith, 1891–1942—Pictorial works.
6. Carmelite Nuns—Germany—Biography—Pictorial
works. 7. Christian martyrs—Germany—Biography—
Pictorial works. 8. Christian philosophers—Germany—
Biography—Pictorial works.
  I. Title.
  BX4705.S814N49   1998
  271'.97102—dc21
  [b]   98–6863
                  CIP

Photo Credits

Page Number	
25	Stadtarchiv Frankfurt
26	Ursula Edelmann, Frankfurt
34 right	Franz Bücheler, Bergzabern
35 upper right	Bildkunst-Verlag Poppe, Bad Kissingen
38 left	Deutsche Luftbild, Hamburg
48, 50 right	Beuroner Kunstverlag
52 above	Kunstverlag Hans Storms, Mönchengladbach
Cover photo and all others	Edith-Stein-Archiv, Cologne

TABLE OF CONTENTS

Translator's Note

I want to thank Sr. Amata Neyer, O.C.D., and ICS Publications for granting me the privilege of translating this carefully researched presentation of Edith Stein in documents and pictures. The gentle image of the saint that emerges in these pages from a time at once much simpler than ours and yet so tragic will be etched in my mind from now on.

I also want to thank Suzanne Batzdorff, Edith Stein's niece, for correcting a few very minor errors in the text and for assistance in translating the documents. As far as possible, I have used existing English translations of Edith Stein's works, with slight modifications as needed.

Waltraut Stein
Decatur, Georgia

Every human life hides a mystery; it is situated in the darkness of the unfathomable. Even though historical research and psychological illumination are essential to every biography, a human life still eludes intellectual penetration. Its authentic expression most nearly comes across in pictures. The first book of the Bible presents us with such an image:

> As the sun went down, Jacob had a dream. He saw a ladder that stood upon the earth and reached up to heaven. On it the angels of God ascended and descended. And behold, the Lord stood at the top and spoke: "I am the Lord, the God of your father Abraham and the God of Isaac. I am with you; I watch over you. Through you all the nations of the earth will be blessed. I will not leave you until I have accomplished what I have promised (Gn 28:12-15 [Translation from Neyer text]).

The image of ascending meant a great deal to Edith Stein. She calls her main work, *Finite and Eternal Being,* "An Attempt to Ascend to the Meaning of Being." Her last work, which remained unfinished, was a study of John of the Cross, the Carmelite Doctor of the Church. As if in anticipation of what was to come, she dedicated every free minute to this holy fellow Carmelite whose life and teachings had only one goal: the "Ascent of Mount Carmel" where God would be encountered.

Let us beware of a misunderstanding here! Images of steps, the ladder, or the mountain peak could remind us of accomplishment, effort, or strength of will. And, in fact, these are necessary. But what is crucial is not accomplished by our exertion. This misunderstanding almost made the mystic and poet, John of the Cross himself, this troubadour of God's love, into a tired ascetic.

And Edith Stein? How often people praised her unusual capacity for unconditional consistency! But it was not the consistency of her logical thought, not the consistency of her strong will, that brought about the consummation in her, but the consistency of her steadfast love. "I will not leave you until I accomplish what I have promised"—so says the Lord (Gn 28:15).

Let us, therefore, return to our biblical image. Jacob lies asleep and dreams. "As the sun went down" (Gn 28:12), in the dark of night, he sees the messengers of God on the steps of the ladder. These are the steps of the growth and development of his inner life; what he saw in his dream was what happened.

Edith Stein's spiritual director, Dr. Raphael Walzer, the Superior of Beuron and her friend for many years, seizes on this same image when he speaks of Edith Stein. He finds her inner life to be thoroughly simple, very deep and calm. At the same time, he perceives her inner life to be full of activity, like a Jacob's ladder (as he says), on which her thoughts, her insights and ideas, her plans and desires ascended and descended as messengers between herself and God.

And such an inner image corresponds to the exterior. For Edith Stein's outer life is also like a path of steps. This means that every segment of her life leads to the next with great logical consistency; every stretch of the path is meaningfully connected to the previous one in order then to continue to the next—to a new place. In a striking way, the segments of Edith Stein's life are bound to places, cities where she lived and grew, learned and taught, where she found joy and sorrow, and finally death.

The photo, taken about 1894, shows Edith Stein's parents and siblings. The picture is a photo montage. After the sudden death of the father, the family members were sorry that they had no family portrait, and so they had a passport photo of the deceased father inserted into the picture. The picture shows (back row from right): Arno, 1879 (Gleiwitz)–1948 (San Francisco); Else, 1876 (Gleiwitz)–1956 (Bogota, Colombia); Siegfried, 1844 (Langendorf)–1893 (Frauenwaldau/ Goschütz); Elfriede, 1881 (Lublinitz)–1943 (Thersesienstadt); Paul 1872 (Gleiwitz)–1943 (Theresienstadt); front row from left: Rosa 1882 (Lublinitz)–1942 (Auschwitz); Auguste Stein, née Courant, 1849 (Lublinitz)–1936 (Breslau); Edith 1891 (Breslau)–1942 (Auschwitz); Erna, 1890 (Lublinitz)–1978 (Davis, California).

"My mother once said," wrote Edith, "that each of her children presented her with a special mystery."

At first the family lived at Kohlenstrasse 13, where Edith was born. Then they moved to Schiesswerderstrasse and shortly thereafter to Jägerstrasse 5, where the family of eight lived for many years in a three and a half room home. At that time, the lumberyard was on Rosenstrasse. Edith spoke much about this lumberyard. All the children of the extended family and the neighborhood were allowed to romp there. Edith Stein considered such a playground to be an important place of formation, a place for one's first activities for proving oneself, and for meetings.

The workers at the lumberyard also belonged to the family. Frau Stein was generous to them, but also a real matriarch to the whole throng. When Frau Stein came from the lumberyard in winter with warm hands, it always seemed to Edith "that all life and all warmth in the house came from her."

▶

BRESLAU

"We are in the world to serve humanity"

Breslau, the capital of Silesia, economic and cultural center of eastern Germany, is the world of Edith Stein's childhood. "I, Edith Stein, was born on October 12, 1891, in Breslau, the daughter of the deceased merchant Siegfried Stein and his wife Auguste, née Courant. I am a Prussian citizen and Jewish."

Frau Auguste Stein used to divide her family into three groups: the boys, the girls, and the "children." The last were the "afterthoughts" Erna and Edith. The two sisters were bound in a special friendship throughout life. Erna became a gynecologist and married a dermatologist, Dr. Hans Biberstein (1898-1965). This photo was taken about 1900 (right Edith, left Erna). Like their older sisters, Erna and Edith went to Victoria School at Ritterplatz, later on Blücherstrasse. It was first a high school for girls [Höhere Töchterschule], then a girls' secondary school [Mädchenlyzeum] and finally a secondary school with a scientific emphasis [Realgymnasium]. By passing an additional examination in Greek, Edith received a diploma from high school that emphasized the humanities.

Edith's parents ran a lumber business. They moved to Breslau in 1889-1890 for economic advancement. Auguste and Siegfried Stein had eleven children of which seven reached adulthood. Shortly after Edith's birth, her father died. Auguste Stein—self-sufficient, proud, goal-oriented—immediately took over the direction of the lumber business and turned the debt-ridden firm into a respected business. She was a devout Jew who headed the household in faithful adherence to the laws. Yet she did not succeed in communicating the richness of Jewish spirituality to her children.

Edith, her mother's favorite, protected and spoiled by brothers and sisters, developed rapidly as a child, sometimes brimming with life, wise beyond her years and saucy, sometimes dreamy, reserved and anxious. The highly gifted little girl found kindergarten dreadful, school inspiring. At the age of fourteen, she suddenly broke off everything. But two years later she developed new enthusiasm. She took private lessons and went back to the *Gymnasium* [high school] from which she graduated with a brilliant record in 1911.

Speaking of the time when she was tired of school, Edith later observed, "I was fed up with learning...." She explains this by the restlessness she felt during her adolescent years and by the philosophical questions that were beginning to emerge. At the same time, the adolescent girl felt with that unerring certainty which we will encounter again and

In 1903 Frau Stein acquired the lumberyard on Matthiasstrasse 151, and in 1910, the roomy house nearby at Michaelisstrasse 38 for her family.

On the gate to the front garden one can see the enameled sign for the medical practice of Dr. Erna Biberstein-Stein. Family members can be seen in the windows of the first floor. As a student, Edith Stein used to walk back and forth before the house gate philosophizing with friends when she came home. This was not to her mother's liking. Later Edith said about this, "Naturally, the people in the neighborhood had no idea that we were immersed in psychological or epistemological problems. But we took every opportunity to say that we did not care what 'they' said or what 'people' thought...."

Edith, Erna, and Gerhard Stein, the son of her oldest brother, Paul. This photo was taken in the Stein family's garden, probably in 1905.

Pages 12 and 13:
Because of her outstanding achievements, Edith Stein was exempted from the oral exam at her high school graduation. The leaving certificate [p. 13, right] was issued on March 3, 1911. The absence of religious instruction [among the subjects listed] is noteworthy. The upplementary exam in Greek on October 26, 1915 is entered at the end of the form.

Städtische Viktoriaschule in Breslau
Studienanstalt der realgymnasialen Richtung

Zeugnis der Reife.

Edith Stein

geboren den 12. Oktober 18 91 zu Breslau, Kreis _____

_____, mosaischer Konfession, Tochter des in Breslau verstorbenen Kaufmanns Siegfried Stein zu _____

Kreis _____, war 3 Jahre auf der realgymnasialen Studienanstalt der Viktoriaschule und zwar ein Jahr in der obersten Klasse.

I. Führung und Aufmerksamkeit:

Die Führung war gut, die Aufmerksamkeit sehr gut. — Von der mündlichen Prüfung wurde sie befreit

II. Kenntnisse und Fertigkeiten.

1. Religionslehre: _____

Gesamturteil: _____

---

2. Deutsch:

Die Klassenleistungen waren stets gut und sehr gut. Auch der Abiturientenaufsatz erhielt das Prädikat gut. Sie besitzt gründliche über den Rahmen der Schule hinausgehende Kenntnisse in der Literaturgeschichte.

Gesamturteil: *sehr gut*

3. Französisch:

Mit sicherem grammatischen Wissen verbindet sie das Sachwissen, Schriftsteller mit recht gutem Verständnis zu lesen. Ihre Leistungen in der Klasse waren daher immer gut, zuweilen auch besser. Die Prüfungsarbeit erhielt das Prädikat gut.

Gesamturteil: *gut*

4. Englisch:

In der Grammatik besitzt sie gute Kenntnisse. Bei der Lektüre zeigte sie prächtliche Auffassung des Textes und Geschick im Übertragen desselben in die Muttersprache.

Gesamturteil: *gut*

5. Lateinisch:

Die Klassenleistungen waren teils gut, teils sehr gut. Die Prüfungsarbeit war gut. Die erworbenen Kenntnisse sind sicher und gründlich.

Gesamturteil: *sehr gut*

6. Geschichte:

Die Klassenleistungen waren sehr gut.

Gesamturteil: *sehr gut*

7. Erdkunde:

Die Klassenleistungen waren gut

Gesamturteil: gut

8. Mathematik:

Die Klassenleistungen waren gut, dem
entsprach auch die schriftliche Prüfungsarbeit.

Gesamturteil: gut

9. Physik:

Die Klassenleistungen sowie die schriftliche
Prüfungsarbeit waren gut.

Gesamturteil: gut

10. Chemie:

Die Klassenleistungen waren sehr gut.

Gesamturteil: gut

11. Turnen: gut

12. Zeichnen: gut

13. Singen: —

Die unterzeichnete Prüfungskommission hat ihr demnach das Zeugnis

der Reife

zuerkannt.

Breslau, den 3 ten März 19 11.

Königliche Prüfungskommission.

Dr. Brinckmann   Königlicher Kommissar.

Dr. Harb   Vertreter des Magistrats.

Prof. H. Roen   Direktor.

Sumpf   Professor.

K. Michel   Professor.

Dr. Olbrich   Professor.

A. Lengert   Professor.

F. Seltz Vorschullehrer.

Fräulein Edith Stein hat sich heute einer Prüfung im Griechischen unterzogen
und diese gut bestanden. Sie hat sich damit das Reifezeugnis eines Gymna-
siums erworben.

Breslau, d. 26. October 1915.

Vorschuldirektor Laudien,
Geheimer Regierungsrat.

13

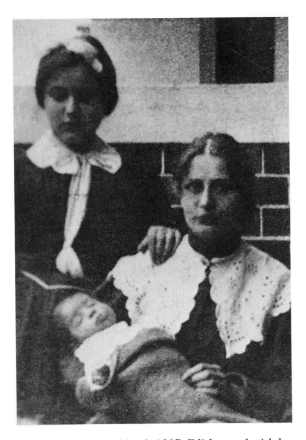

From May 1906 to March 1907, Edith stayed with her oldest sister in Hamburg. Else Stein lived there with her husband, dermatologist Dr. Max Gordon. "Max and Else were completely without faith. There was no religion at all in this house." The photo shows Edith (left) with Else and her second child, Werner. Years later, by means of patient, empathic mediation, Edith was able to rescue the failing marriage of her sister and brother-in-law. The family emigrated in 1939, some to Norway, some to Colombia.

again in Edith Stein that she needs something new. In order to change, she needs to be someplace else. She goes to Hamburg where her oldest sister is expecting her second child and is having marital difficulties. A year later, Edith returns home to Breslau a young lady. She also considers the religious question to be resolved: She has renounced her faith, "deliberately and consciously...." The interruption in Edith's schooling had not only enabled her to master her courses at the gymnasium and her student years in Breslau almost as if they were play; her position in the family also changed completely. The spoiled child became the grown daughter and sister.

But not only that. Edith sets family life increasingly aside. And everyone suffers—but not Edith. She sets forth her life plan in these words: "We are in the world to serve humanity." This is how she expresses her intense ethical idealism. She has a strong sense of social responsibility that is tied to a strong feeling for the solidarity of all people. But this also involves a protest: The interests of her sizable family are no longer hers. A circle of new female and male friends admires and woos her. Her unusual talent for grasping new thoughts and for empathizing with others, her truthfulness, her enthusiasm—all these open to her many relationships and projects, i.e., lectures, seminars, tutoring, participation in student circles, in social and political associations, and organizations.

◄

As a student, Edith often visited this group of children in a home on the Warteberg by Obernigk. Her interest in educational questions of that time also stimulated her to inform herself about social institutions and about educational facilities for the blind, the deaf, or the mentally retarded. The house on the Warteberg was run by sisters from a Protestant nursing order from the mother house at Castle Miechowitz. It was established by Eva von Tiele-Winckler, a member from Bodelschwinghs.

On April 28, 1911, Edith matriculated at Breslau University. She enjoyed the "academic freedom" to the fullest. Since she was not bound to a prescribed curriculum, she took what she wanted to take. However, she later remarked that the lack of a professional direction was also a disadvantage for her education. At the same time, Edith felt "deep gratitude to the state which offered me as a citizen the academic right of free access to the humanities. All the little privileges which our student card ensured..., awakened in me the wish to render my thanks later to the people and the state through my professional work." ►

The "constant exertion of all my powers gave me an exhilarating feeling of living a very full life. I saw myself as a privileged creature. So I lived in the naive self-delusion that everything was all right with me...." No longer did anyone dare to criticize or censure her. Nevertheless, she felt justified in criticizing anyone else, "often in a mocking and ironic tone."

Precisely during this time, however, there arose the first signs of depressive anxieties about life. The reading of a tendentious novel that repelled her propelled her into a period of ennui and mistrust. When she was rescued from being poisoned by gas in an accident at home, she felt deep regret. Edith was alarmed at herself.... But still she bounced back.

▶

Edith Stein loved nature very much and loved to go for long hikes. It was probably during the summer vacation in 1911 that she went on an excursion to Schneekoppe, the highest peak in the Riesengebirge. This picture shows Erna Stein at right, Edith below. The other young ladies are friends.

This picture from the year 1913 shows four of the Stein sisters after a tennis game. From left: Rosa, Erna, Frieda, and (right) Edith. Edith was not only exceptionally gifted in the humanities, but she also received good grades in drawing and gymnastics in school. She was an excellent dancer and enjoyed tobogganing and rowing.

Top left: *During the summer of 1911, Edith spent the vacation with her circle of friends in Gross-Aupa, a Bohemian village. The picture shows her in the middle with her hair pinned over her ears. The best thing about this vacation for Edith was the evenings, when people made plans for the future, raised the problem of dual professions, and spoke about their ideals, "which we wanted to realize by our work in the world."*

Top right: *This photo was also taken during summer vacation in 1911. Edith is at the right in the last row; in front is her future brother-in-law, Hans Biberstein. Edith calls him a rare bird among the students, because he was strongly for the full equality of women. The whole group were members of the Prussian Organization for Women's Suffrage.*

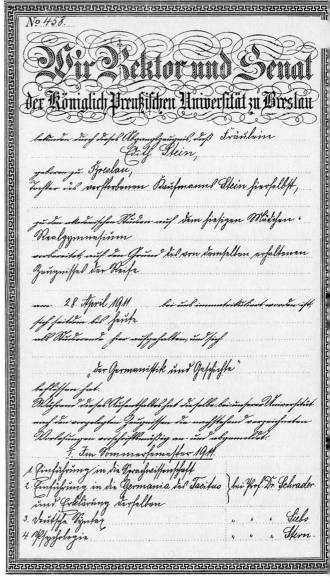

This is the novel [Helmut Harringer, *by Hermann Popert*] that so deeply troubled and impressed Edith Stein. It portrays student life from a side that Edith did not know at all, and which was entirely against her idealism: with alcoholism, duels, and immorality. Possibly the insistent defense of the Nordic race also repelled her. The Bach festival celebrated in 1912 in Breslau finally pulled her out of her deep depression.

Leaving certificate from the University of Breslau.

18

GÖTTINGEN
"Glimpse into new worlds"

No city had more meaning for Edith Stein during the first half of her life than Göttingen. Here she was, "almost without noticing it, gradually transformed." Edith had felt at home in the atmosphere of university life in Breslau, giving and receiving at the same time. And yet all at once she experienced what she had come to love as confining. "Here I would have been able to add a great deal to my knowledge," she writes, "but I longed to go elsewhere."

She had mainly studied psychology for four semesters in Breslau and had repeatedly come across the name of the philosopher Edmund Husserl and his phenomenological method. For Husserl, this method is not a philosophy about content but considers "the things themselves." It ignores what is merely factual and seeks to grasp the essence of "that which appears." "The attention is turned away from the 'subject' and to 'things' themselves; perception again appeared as reception, deriving its laws from objects, not from a designation which imposes laws on objects," writes Edith. Her step from psychology to phenomenology confirmed for her that the former "lacked the necessary foundation of clarified basic concepts," while the latter "consisted

Edith Stein went to Göttingen because of Husserl. Their friendship continued until Husserl's death. Edmund Husserl was born in 1859 in Prossnitz in Moravia. He studied in Leipzig, Berlin, and Vienna, came to philosophy through mathematics, and qualified as a university lecturer in Halle before becoming a professor in Göttingen. In 1900 and 1901, the two volumes of his Logical Investigations *appeared, and in 1912 his* Ideas. *These were the works that made Husserl's phenomenological method world-famous.*

Edith arrived in Göttingen on April 17, 1913. The first time she strolled around the city she noticed the many nameplates on the houses in which former prominent personages had lived. There is now also such a nameplate in Göttingen for Edith Stein on the house that was her first domicile there, at Lange Geismarstrasse 2. The house belonged to the painter Wilhelm Gille. The Cultural Committee decided to put the nameplate there on November 9, 1973.

precisely of such work of clarification in which one forged the conceptual framework for oneself." She made her decision quickly. She had to go to Göttingen for the summer semester of 1913! And she was enthralled by the new ideas that awaited her there.

Half at odds with herself, Edith knew deep down that there was more to this than an interesting semester away. In fact, she would meet people in Göttingen and work through experiences that crossed her path like divine messengers, still unrecognized. Yet these messengers would lead her onward "to confront the most important decision of my life," she would later write. She developed relationships with people that began to open "a hitherto totally unknown world." This was the world of faith, for Edith admittedly at first only a "realm of phenomena." However, it had to be worthy of serious consideration, since people superior to her lived in it, people she admired. And her relationship with these people had "more depth and beauty than my former student friendships. For the first time, I was not the one to lead or to be sought after."

Edith clearly sensed the extent to which the time in Göttingen "is the beginning of a new phase of my life." For the first time in her life, she encountered problems she has chosen for herself that pushed her resources to the limit and resisted being mastered by reason and will. She was no longer able to shake off loneliness and discouragement; she was exhausted; she began to experience despair, yes, and even thoughts of death.

In the meantime, the World War broke out. It was the summer of 1914. Edith was wide awake to the great event. Without reservation she intended to subordinate her life to it. She went to the Red Cross, took the test to be an assistant, and worked feverishly in a typhoid military hospital at the Carpathian front.

◀

Edith credited the "Philosophical Society," the narrow circle of serious students of Husserl, with the greatest stimulation she received in Göttingen. This photo was taken in the year 1912, the year before Edith came to Göttingen. From left it shows Jean Hering, Schröder (first name not available), Adolf Reinach, Hans Lipps, Theodor Conrad, Max Scheler, Alexander Koyré, Siegfried Hamburger, Hedwig Martius, Rudolf Clemens, Gustav Hübener, Alfred von Sybel. Edith Stein was later a friend of nearly all of these. Of particular meaning for her were her encounters with Max Scheler, Adolf Reinach, Hans Lipps, and Hedwig Martius. Scheler, who was at that time still an enthusiastic Catholic, gave guest lectures in Göttingen. For the first time, Edith encountered the world of Catholic faith in a thinker of rank.

▶

The day after she arrived in Göttingen Edith sought out Adolf Reinach. Originally a student of Theodor Lipps in Munich, he moved to Göttingen because of Husserl's works and had founded the "Philosophical Society" there with Theodor Conrad. During Edith Stein's time he was an outside lecturer and Husserl's right hand in dealing with students. For a short time he lived with Anne (née Stettenheimer) in a most happy marriage, which was ended by his untimely death. (He was killed in 1917 at the western front.) Edith very much dreaded the encounter with the young wife when she was asked to sort out his literary remains. However, Anne Reinach, who had a short time earlier been converted to Protestantism with her husband (both were Jews), remained self-possessed and did not break down. In her presence Edith experienced for the first time the strength that faith in the saving crucifixion of Jesus could give to suffering people.

The most difficult time for Edith in Göttingen was the winter semester of 1913-1914. She wanted to dedicate herself to working on her doctoral dissertation with the theme On the Problem of Empathy. But this was not to be. "I gradually worked myself into real despair.... I could no longer cross the street without wishing that a car would run over me...and I would not come out alive...." She finally decided to talk with Adolf Reinach. His understanding response slowly brought her to her senses again and enabled her to return to her intellectual work until the outbreak of war interrupted it the following summer.

In the Cadet Academy in Moravian Weisskirchen, which was converted to a typhoid military hospital, there lay thousands of very ill soldiers. Auguste Stein tried to forbid Edith to go there. "You will not go with my consent!" "Then I must do so without your consent," retorted Edith.

The nursing staff in Moravian Weisskirchen occasionally put on a party. It was harmless, but Edith Stein (in the foreground), "Nurse Edith," was uncomfortable. "I thought about my patients," she writes, and adds that she was also not used to cigarettes and strong coffee.

23

Even before she was called up to the service to which she felt impatiently drawn, she took her *Staatsexam* or final exam on her course work in Göttingen. After being discharged from her medical service, she reviewed her Greek and then began her year as an assistant instructor in Breslau. First of all she wanted to serve as a substitute for a very ill secondary school instructor; but at the same time she also wanted to reassure her mother and siblings that she had now set out on a clear path.

Edith occasionally went on a Sunday excursion with the upper secondary class at the Victoria School where she began her year as an assistant instructor, "...like real wanderers with cooking utensils and guitars." Edith Stein at the very top of the picture.

FREIBURG
"To obey is something I cannot do"

In April 1916, Husserl, the "Master," was appointed to Freiburg University. This meant that Edith, too, had to go there for her doctoral examination. She had never been in southwestern Germany and now looked forward to something new.

En route, she met her Göttingen student friend Hans Lipps and became acquainted with Frankfurt and Heidelberg. What Edith decades later could still relate of all this shows that what she encountered as evidence of Christian life not only caused her to reflect seriously but also moved her deeply. Hans Lipps tells her about a young phenomenologist who had converted: "'Are you by chance also among them?' — 'No, I don't belong.' I almost said, 'unfortunately not,'" as she later recounted the conversation.

In July 1916, Edith Stein interrupts her trip to Freiburg in Frankfurt. She is more impressed with an encounter in the Cathedral than by the monuments to Goethe at the Römerberg and the Hirsch cemetery. A woman who had been shopping came into the empty church and knelt silently in a pew. Edith Stein never forgot this. In synagogues and in Protestant churches, she had only seen people who prayed during services. But here someone came into the empty church "as if to an intimate conversation."

When Edith returned to Breslau, she had passed the exam with highest honors. This was to be expected. Moreover, she had in her pocket an agreement with Husserl that in the fall she would work as his academic assistant. This was unexpected. Edith was happy. Now she could give up school teaching and make her interests and special gifts her daily work. But the year and a half with Husserl was to be a difficult time. Professor and assistant each had very different ideas of how they were to work together. Edith wanted to help the brilliant professor to continue in his investigations, to finish the new work that people were

In Freiburg Edith noticed that Husserl found himself in a difficult situation. He needed an assistant, but his students were all on the battlefield. Once when Edith was walking with him over the old Frederick Bridge, she offered to help him, and Husserl agreed, joyfully surprised. Writes Edith, "I don't know which one of us was happier."

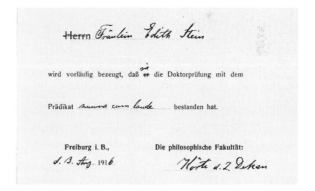

On July 31, 1916, the Albert-Ludwig University of Freiburg notified Edith of the date and time for her oral doctoral examination.

On the same day as the exam, August 3, 1916, the chairman of the philosophy department gave Edith a first report that she had passed summa cum laude— with highest distinction.

Good friends had advised Edith to seek housing not in the city of Freiburg but in the suburb of Günterstal. Even though preparing for exams, Edith took long hikes in the Black Forest with her sister Erna and with friends who visited them.

Edith found a quiet room suitable for study and a friendly landlady in this house at Dorfstrasse 4.

Edith Stein's doctoral diploma. ▶

expecting from him in professional circles, to prepare long awaited publications for the press. She attended all the master's lectures, so that she could interpret his concepts for those listeners who were unfamiliar with them. For this purpose she conducted her own introductory seminar. "Strictly ABC instruction," she said about this, "but even so it is fun." (Incidentally, famous scholars came out of this "philosophical kindergarten.")

However, everything did not materialize as she had envisoned. Husserl had her examine and revise piles of manuscripts in shorthand. But then, instead of using what she had put in order he began something unexpected and then again abruptly dropped what he had

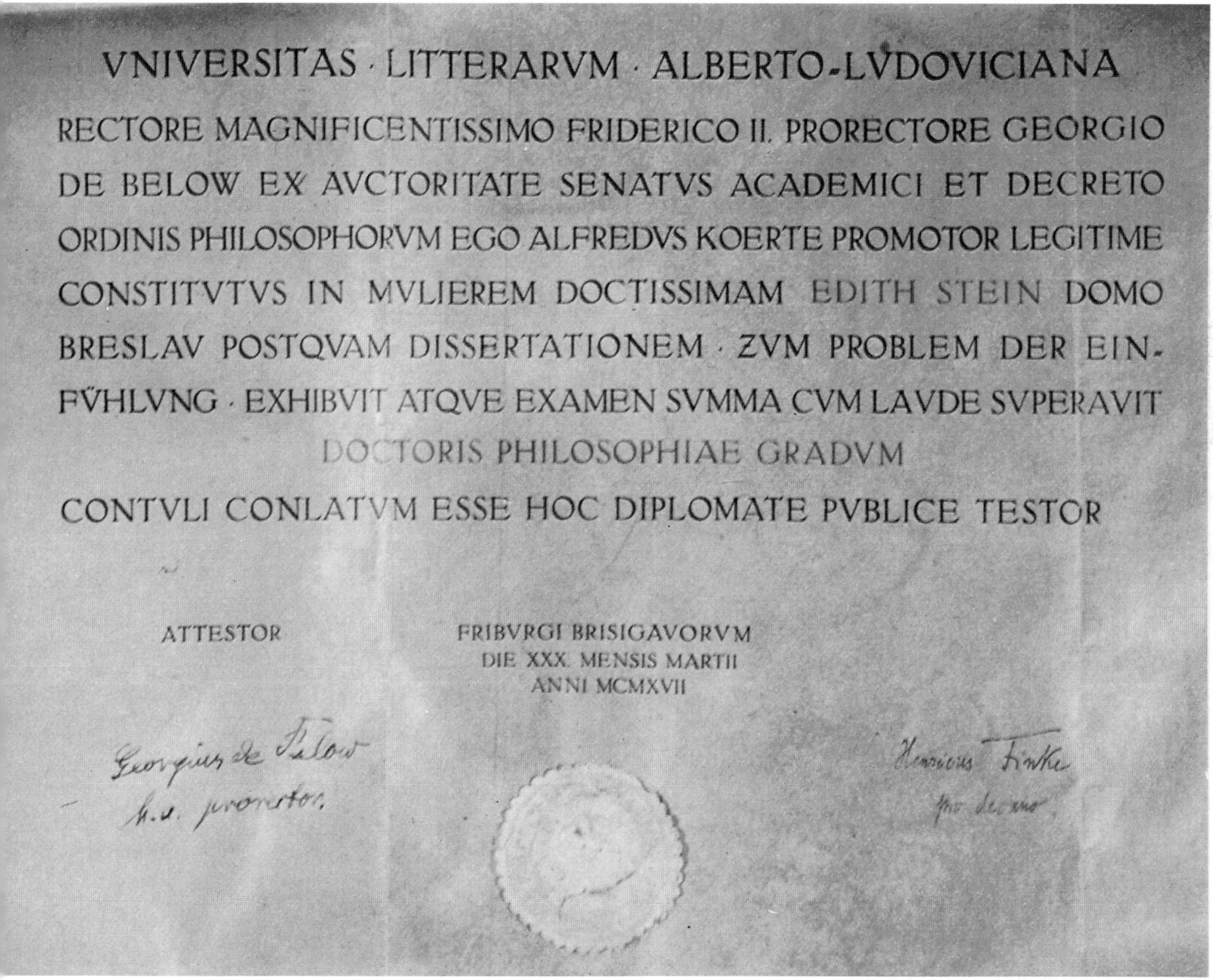

VNIVERSITAS · LITTERARVM · ALBERTO-LVDOVICIANA

RECTORE MAGNIFICENTISSIMO FRIDERICO II. PRORECTORE GEORGIO DE BELOW EX AVCTORITATE SENATVS ACADEMICI ET DECRETO ORDINIS PHILOSOPHORVM EGO ALFREDVS KOERTE PROMOTOR LEGITIME CONSTITVTVS IN MVLIEREM DOCTISSIMAM EDITH STEIN DOMO BRESLAV POSTQVAM DISSERTATIONEM · ZVM PROBLEM DER EIN- FVHLVNG · EXHIBVIT ATQVE EXAMEN SVMMA CVM LAVDE SVPERAVIT

DOCTORIS PHILOSOPHIAE GRADVM

CONTVLI CONLATVM ESSE HOC DIPLOMATE PVBLICE TESTOR

ATTESTOR

FRIBVRGI BRISIGAVORVM
DIE XXX. MENSIS MARTII
ANNI MCMXVII

Georgius de Below
h. t. promotor.

Henricus Finke
pro decano.

begun. Also, external demands continually got in the way; the death of his son and the misery of war limited the scholar's energy. In addition, Edith found it impossible to consider doing work of her own in this situation.

During this time she wrote to a student friend, "Pray for me...." It is the first evidence that prayer had begun to mean something for her again.

Gradually Edith got the impression that Husserl was more interested in fulfilling personal projects than in working jointly on technical matters with her. His instructions became more and more limited to the organization of manuscripts for which she could see no necessity. When one day Husserl gave her such a task with detailed instructions, she

At the beginning of October 1916, Edith began her assistantship with Husserl. She stayed in Freiburg until the fall of 1918. Husserl gave her a handwritten testimony which concluded with a recommendation for qualification as a university lecturer: "Should the academic profession become open to women, I would recommend Dr. Stein immediately and most warmly for qualification as a university lecturer."

asked to be relieved of this work. Husserl let her go, later writing her a glowing recommendation, and proposed her for qualification as a university lecturer. Edith also continued to respect the brilliant man. For her, he "will always remain the master, whose image cannot be marred by any human weakness."

BERGZABERN
"That's my secret"

In looking back on the year 1916, Edith Stein once spoke of "the remarkable zigzag line of my life up to now." By this she meant to say that taking one step forward and another step back, one step up and another down were not arbitrary, but were divinely guided until the next place in life could be reached.

Toward the end of 1918, Edith Stein left Freiburg for good. She had been in Göttingen early in the year, and the following year found her there several more times. She had finished a long work and was trying to qualify as a university lecturer, but without success.

She spent the year 1920 in Breslau, giving private lectures at her family's home and giving courses in the public high school. She wrote, "I was on tenterhooks. I was passing through a personal crisis that I could not resolve in our house." She also felt ill physically, "probably as a result of the spiritual conflicts which I endured in complete secrecy and without any human support."

At about this time it must have become clear to her that Hans Lipps was taking his own

In their hospitable home in Bergzabern in the Palatinate, Hedwig and Theodor Conrad received many of the young phenomenologists to work with them and for the lively exchange of ideas. The Conrads' guest book shows that Edith Stein spent most of the year 1921 there. When she needed more space, she moved from the guest room to the attic chamber. The house was at Eisbrünnelweg (today renamed Neubergstrasse) 16.

The Conrads, both philosophers, earned their living in part by cultivating a fruit orchard. "During the day they worked there with the plants," an eyewitness reports, "in the evenings they philosophized." The photo shows Hedwig Conrad-Martius working in the fruit orchard (about 1921).

In the early summer of 1921, Edith immersed herself in the autobiography of the mystic and Doctor of the Church Teresa of Avila. Her occupation with this work brings to an end a long struggle in her and allows her to reach the decision to enter the Catholic Church. Edith later reports that she was prepared for this decision by her encounters with Max Scheler and Anne Reinach.

way, which would forever be separate from hers. This fate deepened in her questions that had long been arising and could no longer be pushed aside. These were the questions: What shape am I going to give my life? Where can I find God? She again knew with unerring certainty that she had not only to discover the answers but to live and act on them.

In March 1921, Edith set out from Breslau for Göttingen and from there for

Edith stayed in the family home in Breslau from the beginning of August to the end of October 1921. Her sister Erna was expecting her first child, and Edith assisted her in her medical practice and in the household. At the same time, she asked her sister to let her mother know of her forthcoming conversion. Erna writes about this, "I knew that this was one of the most difficult tasks that I had ever confronted."

Edith already attended Mass every morning in Breslau during the months before her baptism. She arose very early and left the house without a sound. Nevertheless, Frau Stein often awakened; she was filled with anxious premonitions that Edith would convert to the Catholic Church. Later, too, Edith attended services at St. Michael whenever she was in Breslau.

Bergzabern to the place where her friends, the philosoper couple Theodor and Hedwig Conrad-Martius, lived, both students of Husserl. It was there "in the summer of 1921 that the *Life* of our Holy Mother Teresa happened to fall into my hands" and her "long search for the true faith came to an end."

How could this happen? Edith replied, "That's my secret." When people take such steps, the call of God and human decision

◀

Auguste Stein, Edith's mother, suffered deeply over the conversion of her daughter to the Catholic Church. Her consolation was her granddaughter Susanne, Erna Biberstein's first child, born a short time before.

mysteriously intermingle. Edith herself believed that she was prepared for the understanding of Teresa that resolved all her doubts by people whose deep faith demanded her further reflection and searching. For years she had looked for truth philosophically as a scholar. It was the "truth of things," the "things themselves," the objects. Now in Teresa of Avila she was filled with the truth of love that is not knowledge, but relationship. Teresa lived in mystical friendship with God and with him whom God had sent, Jesus Christ.

On January 1, 1922, through baptism Edith Stein was received into the Catholic Church. At that time, it was on this day that people reflected on Jesus' circumcision. This is the only Jewish rite that was a high feast day in the liturgical calendar of the Church.

The baptismal font in the parish church of St. Martin where Edith Stein received the sacrament of new birth on New Year's Day, 1922. Her sponsor was her friend, Hedwig Conrad-Martius, whose white wedding gown Edith wore as a baptismal dress.

Dean Eugen Breitling (born 1851 in Böhl, died 1931 in Bergzabern), who baptized Edith Stein.

Above right: *The interior of the Catholic parish church in Bad Bergzabern where Edith was baptized. Today a number of memorial tablets there commemorate the event.*

▶

Entry in the St. Martin baptismal book in Bergzabern:
"...baptizata est Editha Stein, ...quae a Judaismo in religionem catholicam transivit, bene instructa et disposita." At her baptism, Edith took the two Christian names of Theresia and Hedwig. She received her first holy Communion on the same morning at St. Martin.

At the bottom left of the baptismal document one can read a later entry refering to Edith Stein's vows as a Carmelite. Edith often said that it had been her decision from the day of her baptism to enter the order of St. Teresa when the time was right.

SPEYER
"I have a small, simple truth to express"

Edith returned to Breslau ten months after her baptism (in October 1922), but not for long. On February 2, 1922, she had been confirmed in the private chapel of the bishop of Speyer. She had made the acquaintance of the Dominican convent of St. Magdalene and its schools through their Vicar General, and now accepted a position as a teacher there.

A number of considerations led to this decision. In her particular situation, it was desirable to be independent of her family as well as to become familiar with church life in Catholic surroundings. At the same time, the convent home enabled her to spend quiet hours of meditation in the private chapel and to pray the Divine Office with the sisters. Along with service in the classroom, it also offered opportunities for scholarly work.

After her conversion, Edith was at first convinced that the new life into which she had been baptized required the greatest possible detachment from everything "earthly." Slowly she grew more deeply into Christ and understood that she, like Christ, is sent to human beings, called to carry the divine life into the world with him. "I am only an instrument of the Lord," she writes, "I would like to lead those who come to me to him." Her teaching

Bishop Ludwig Sebastian (born in Frankenstein in 1862, died in Speyer in 1943), who confirmed Edith.

The confirmation certificate made out when Edith Stein entered Carmel. The printed form contains an error: Edith was not confirmed in the cathedral in Speyer but in the bishop's private chapel.

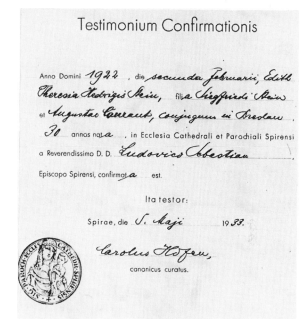

Testimonium Confirmationis

Anno Domini *1922*, die *secunda februarii*, Edith Theresia Hedwigis Stein, filia Siegfridi Stein et Augustae Courant, conjugum in Breslau, *30* annos nata, in Ecclesia Cathedrali et Parochiali Spirensi a Reverendissimo D. D. *Ludovico Sebastian*, Episcopo Spirensi, confirmata est.

Ita testor:

Spirae, die *5. Maji* 19 *33*.

Carolus Höfer,

canonicus curatus.

On February 2, 1922 Edith was confirmed in the private chapel of the bishop of Speyer, to whose diocese Bergzabern belongs.

In Speyer, Edith found a wise advisor and cherished friend in Vicar General Josef Schwind. After his death in 1927, Edith Stein devoted a detailed obituary to him in the diocesan bulletin.

37

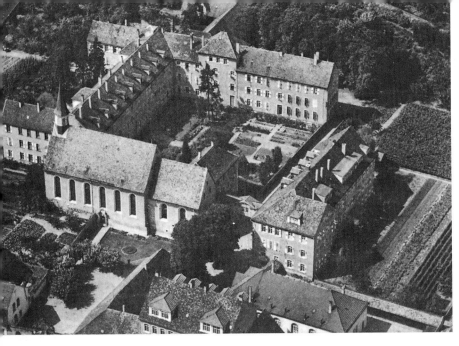

Through Vicar General Schwind, Edith Stein became acquainted with the Dominican convent of St. Magdalene in Speyer. The convent with its school rooms and dormitory became home and workplace for her for eight years. She made friends with a number of the nuns, friendships that lasted until her death. She taught Latin to some of the postulants and novices. When the weather was good, a little flag appeared in "Miss Doctor's" window indicating that she was awaiting them for lessons in the garden.

▶

So that she could pray in the convent church of St. Magdalene unseen and undisturbed, Edith Stein made use of this corner behind a pillar. The door (only half of which is visible) leads to the presbytery of the church. Thus Edith could seek out her prayer bench inconspicuously at any time and had an unrestricted view of the high altar. Part of her spiritual life consisted of repeatedly retreating into stillness and praying whenever her other tasks enabled her to do so. She also encouraged others in this inner prayer. It is precisely people with many obligations and who are fully involved, she argued, who need such communion with themselves where God dwells in us. Edith teaches us that we do not need to be in a church to do this; one can catch one's breath spiritually anywhere.

Below: Edith Stein as instructor in the garden of the St. Magdalene's Convent with boarding students wearing the prescribed uniform. (One seldom saw her without books, but never with a purse or briefcase!)

Edith Stein had this photo taken during the summer vacation of 1926 in Breslau for a student teacher in Speyer.

Edith Stein among her students. "Today's younger generation," she wrote later in a letter to a nun who was a school teacher, "has been through so many crises that they can no longer understand us; but we must try to understand them.... "

style is certainly the one customary at that time; her innate diffidence and her tendency never completely to overcome severity in her demands—of herself and others—were not eradicated. And everyone—students as well as sisters—noticed her increasing closeness to God in the depths of her heart, and the sincerity of her devotion permitted trust and friendship to develop around her. The same is also definitely true in regard to her loved ones in Breslau where she spent her summer vacation every year.

The Catholic public, too, began to notice Edith Stein. More and more frequently she was invited to speak at feastday events and meetings. Frequently she put herself at the

Edith Stein during her time in Speyer.

disposal of the large Catholic organizations—teachers' associations, women's groups, academic organizations. She conducted extension courses for young male and female teachers, wrote articles and reviews, and spoke on the radio.

As a broadly educated woman, Edith Stein was also a multi-faceted speaker, even though her main and surely favorite topic was the education of women. For her, liturgical and eucharistic devotion were the starting point, path, and goal of religious formation, for men as well. More than fifty years ago Edith Stein expressed thoughts in this area that are still very much worthy of consideration today. She does not even avoid the "difficult and much debated question of the priesthood for women." "In terms of dogma," she said in a lecture, "it seems to me that such an implementation by the Church, until now unheard of, cannot be forbidden." One must add that she herself did not feel called to this path. "Whether ordained or not ordained, whether man or woman, everyone is called to follow Christ." That was her path. But she is also convinced that "only the most purely developed male and female uniqueness can yield the highest attainable likeness to God. Only in this fashion can there be brought about the strongest interpenetration of all earthly and divine life."

The "small, simple truth" that she had to express was the relationship of love to Jesus Christ, and at his hand she found the way to the Father in heaven.

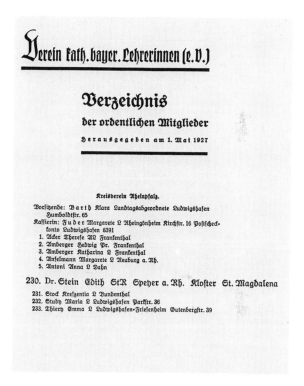

Of course, Edith Stein was a member of the Association of Catholic Teachers of Bavaria (later Germany). She spoke at their general conventions on a number of occasions. Maria Schmitz (1875-1962), appointed by the State as President of this Association for many years, esteemed and promoted Edith Stein. Later she was also instrumental in obtaining for her the teaching position in Münster.

J. H. KARDINAL NEWMAN
BRIEFE
UND TAGEBÜCHER
bis zum Übertritt zur Kirche

1801–1845

Mit Einleitungen
von
FRANCIS BACCHUS UND HENRY TRISTRAM

Übertragen
von
Dr. EDITH STEIN

Herausgegeben
von
P. ERICH PRZYWARA S. J.

1928

THEATINER VERLAG MÜNCHEN

DES HL. THOMAS VON AQUINO
UNTERSUCHUNGEN ÜBER DIE
WAHRHEIT
(QUAESTIONES DISPUTATAE DE VERITATE)

IN DEUTSCHER ÜBERTRAGUNG
VON
EDITH STEIN

MIT EINEM GELEITWORT
VON
MARTIN GRABMANN

I. BAND
(QUAESTIO 1–13)

VERLAG VON
OTTO BORGMEYER / BUCHHANDLUNG / BRESLAU
1931

During her years in Speyer, Edith Stein not only taught but also worked as a writer. In spite of her full schedule as a teacher, she was able to complete two major works along with many articles. She even translated a volume of letters and diaries by Cardinal Newman into German. Husserl's student Dietrich von Hildebrand had brought her to the attention of the Jesuit scholar Erich Przywara.

Edith Stein's greatest work in Speyer was her two-volume translation of St. Thomas. Looking back, she said about this undertaking: "…I considered it practically a miracle that the work was completed and —in spite of all it lacked—nevertheless became what it is. For it came from hours snatched out of a full school schedule and a number of other obligations."

At a lecture on St. Elizabeth of Thuringia on May 30, 1931, in St. Elizabeth's jubilee year. Edith Stein spoke eleven times at celebrations of the Saint's seven hundredth anniversary. It was important to her to instill great examples of the Christian life into the hearts of her audience.

"Other obligations" were, for example, lectures again and again. The most significant was probably the presentation in 1930 in Salzburg on "The Ethos of Woman's Vocations." She spoke as the only woman to the large general convention of Catholic Academic Associations. The Salzburg Higher Education Weeks resulted from this organization.

◀

Edith Stein gave continuing education courses for the young women already serving as school teachers. They all sat in her room on the floor around her. Edith introduced them to current political events and contemporary social problems. This was also something entirely new at that time.

▶

Edith Stein wanted not only to convey to her students the facts prescribed by the lesson plan; she also had in mind the comprehensive formation of women. She set for herself a twofold task for the education of young ladies: Those put in her care were to receive the strength to form their lives according to the spirit of Christ. On the other hand, they were also to become familiar with the tasks that would confront them later in their marriages and professions. Edith Stein was ahead of her time when, for example, she wrote to a nun, "…It really will no longer do to send girls out into the world without sexual education…."

When Edith said goodbye to Speyer, she left many dismayed young people behind. However, she did not see this departure as an inner separation: "The circle of people that I consider mine," she writes at about this time, "has so greatly increased over the years that it is completely impossible to stay in touch with them in the usual ways. But I have other means and ways to keep ties alive.... This continuous bond with all those who have been a part of my life is an essential component of my life...." Edith asked her former students to keep her in their prayers for the new tasks that lay before her: "I continually have to deal with very difficult things," she writes to one of them from Vienna, "and I am always glad to know that many of you continue to think about me and help me by remembering me in prayer...."

◀

On March 26, 1931, Edith Stein said goodbye to Speyer. "I was with the Dominicans in Speyer for eight years as a teacher and was inwardly bound to the whole convent," Edith was later to write about this time. She once said smilingly that she did not take herself very seriously as a teacher so that she could take the students entrusted to her and her pedagogical duties all the more seriously. When she left Speyer, she knew how hard it would be for her to pray and work outside a convent environment. But she had learned "to engage in scholarship as a service to God." St. Thomas Aquinas was her teacher in this.

Bescheinigung.
==================

Fräulein Dr. Edith S t e i n war von Ostern 1923
bis Ostern 1931 an unserer Lehrerinnenbildungsanstalt und
am Lyzeum als Lehrerin für deutsche Sprache und Geschichte
tätig. Neben einem reichen Wissen besitzt Fräulein Dr. Stein
eine gründliche philosophische Bildung und erteilte daher
wahrhaft bildenden Unterricht. In ihrer religiös-sittlichen
Lebensführung war sie ihren Schülerinnen ein leuchtendes
Vorbild. Den Junglehrerinnen war sie für deren berufliche
Fortbildung eine vorzügliche Führerin.

Speyer, den 11. Mai 1933.
Lehrerinnenbildungsanstalt der Dominikanerinnen
zu St. Magdalena:

Schw. M. Scholastica Eiswirth, O.P.

Leiterin.

Edith Stein very much enjoyed living and working with the nuns of St. Magdalene. The high respect the Dominicans also had for their "Fräulein Doctor" is evidenced by the director's testimony.

BEURON
"Like the vestibule of heaven"

There is an interval of more than twelve years between Edith Stein's decision to convert (1921) and her entrance into the convent (1933). This was a significant time in the life of the church in Germany. Believing Christians involved in the church had begun to shake off the ghetto mentality which for a long time had cut off Catholics from political and cultural life. Their enthusiastic awakening and the desire for renewal must have found a strong response in the convert. Edith Stein recognized the growing significance of the large Catholic women's organizations and found herself in league with them in their concern for the education of girls and the formation of women. Those were the years during which the Catholic youth organizations (Burg Rothenfels, Romano Guardini), the large organizations of priests (Ludwig Wolker) or the Catholic Union of Academics (Franz Xavier Münch) latched onto the liturgical movement with great enthusiasm and made it their own.

We must keep in mind that the church into which Edith Stein was baptized—after an authentic personal decision—was a church in which countless people never matured into a faith for which they themselves took responsibility. It was much more common to be a "cradle Catholic" and to grow up taking the church for granted. Now the liturgical movement had arisen from the decision to open up to the people anew the church's ancient treasures for living. It had recognized that there is no life of faith in the church unless each individual is united with Christ. And for this to occur there had to be a dynamic encounter with the risen Lord. Then people could participate in his commission: go into the world, into every facet of it—spiritual, social, professional, political.

After the death of Vicar General Josef Schwind in Speyer, Edith became acquainted with the archabbey of Beuron. The Jesuit scholar Erich Przywara had recommended it to her. Thus the young superior Fr. Raphael Walzer now became her director and her friend.

Beuron, with its liturgical life, its emanation of culture, its atmosphere of the essential, with its highly talented, visionary superior, became her chosen home. For Edith, who disliked all luxury, Beuron is "like the vestibule of heaven." Its completely scheduled daily life, its work and duties one after another, converged around a middle point like the spokes of a wheel. From there outward the circle of its full life found its support as well as its inspiration. Beuron, with its monastic life ordered around prayer and worship, gave her inner peace and an outward orientation. And yet, the vestibule is not a place where one can live forever. Even Beuron was for Edith a step on the ladder of her life.

Edith Stein saw the celebration of the liturgy as an encounter with the Lord. This was what she meant when she said repeatedly: To follow the Lord; to receive him in the deepest recesses of one's heart; to share in Christ's ongoing mystical life; to belong to him in free surrender; to be bound with Christ in constant living communion. Edith Stein wanted to help many people attain these goals in life, and she saw in the liturgical year and the celebration of its great mysteries a path on which the Lord allows himself to be encountered. He is there for us in those places so that he can speak with us and we with him. The result should be a cooperation between him and us, a perpetual dialogue in friendship with God.

God is the One who has become human. Those who want to be bound to God must share in divine and human life, must partake of suffering, darkness, helplessness, and finally death. "The path for each of us, for all of humanity" is to cross the gate of death with Christ in order to reach with him the joy of resurrection. This "central mystery of our faith" was for Edith the "pivotal point of world history."

Several times a day Edith made her way in Beuron over this wooden bridge to the abbey to attend the daily office of the monks. But she also often spent long hours in the abbey church in silent meditation.

The "house by the wooden bridge," the Mayer Guest House, in which Edith usually lived when she was in Beuron.

From 1928 until she entered the cloister, Edith Stein spent the great feast days, such as Holy Week and Easter week, in Beuron. During Edith Stein's time the superior of the Benedictines there was Fr. Raphael Walzer (born 1888 in Ravensburg, died 1966 in Heidelberg). From his pen came important statements about Edith Stein: "I have seldom met a person in whom so many and such laudable characteristics were united. At the same time, she remained entirely a woman with tender, almost motherly sensitivities. Mystically gifted, she was unpretentious with simple people, scholarly with scholars, a seeker with seekers, I would almost say a sinner with sinners."

Edith Stein's first entry in the guestbook of the Mayer family.

49

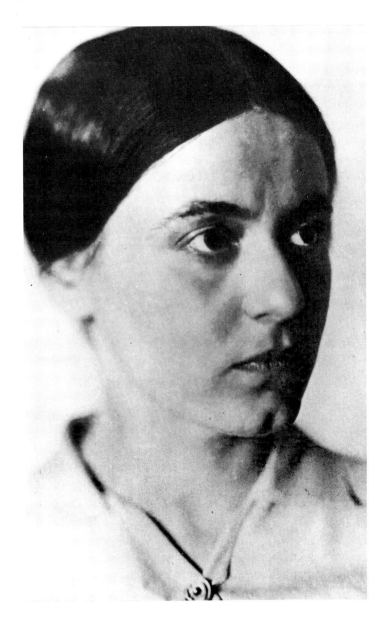

Edith Stein at 40 years of age (1931). "She was probably the first one," commented Archabbot Raphael Walzer, "who would have smiled at the pious exaggerations of her admirers."

When Edith attended the Benedictines' daily office, she joyfully prayed everything with them from her breviary. But she would not accept that only the divine office was "the prayer of the Church," that only the liturgy was worship. "All authentic prayer," she writes, "is the prayer of the Church.... The mystical stream that flows through all centuries is no spurious tributary that has strayed from the prayer life of the Church, it is its deepest life" [The Hidden Life, p. 15—Trans.].

MÜNSTER
"Where my limits lie"

After eight years as a school teacher in Speyer, it became clear to Edith Stein that in the long run she could not combine teaching with scholarly work. So at Easter she gave up her school position at St. Magdalene's convent in order, first of all, to complete her long work, *Act and Potency.*

Her professional future was still obscure. New attempts to quality as a professor ran aground; even other prospects for a career as a scholar came to nothing. At the same time, Edith was filled with complete certainty "that things are as they should be." Then, through the intervention of the Association of Catholic Female Teachers, she was offered a position as a lecturer by the German Institute for Scientific Pedagogy in Münster. Thus, she moved there in February 1932.

Edith Stein begins her work as lecturer in Münster with the summer semester of 1932. Political events already cast their advancing shadows. The young people with whom Edith Stein lives and works are guided by her strong religiosity and the reliability of her worldview.

In Münster, Edith Stein occupied two simple rooms in the student residence Collegium Marianum, in which most of the residents were nuns who were students. Sisters from the Society of Our Lady looked after the house and its inhabitants. They said later that the new lecturer often spent many hours in the house chapel.

Edith Stein was only able to work as a lecturer for one year. Much happened during this year. In the first place, she was busy settling into her work. She developed contacts with the other lecturers as well as with professors and students of the university. Along with her class work, she had to deal with public presentations, professional organizations, discussion evenings, many extra lectures, and a growing correspondence. Her superior expertise, her uncompromising advocacy of the Catholic standpoint, together with her great personal simplicity, ensured her the confidence of many people.

But there was something else affecting her more deeply than all of this. Her scholarly work had drawn the highest praise from specialists, but also bitter criticism from others. Like all great thinkers, Edith Stein was particularly sensitive to the gap between her capacity and the task. Association with people "who are totally caught up in their life's work, who have been educated for it with technical thoroughness

In this lecture hall in the Collegium Marianum, Edith also gave lectures for the residents of the house. Before she left Münster, the nuns and the students gave a musicale in her honor as a festive farewell evening.

and have grown up in it," made her feel the weight of what she has missed. She seemed to see the necessity of beginning philosophical and theological studies completely anew, from the bottom up, and she also knew that this was no longer possible in her circumstances. She lamented that she had lost the sense of modern life and was afraid that she would not find her connection again, and would be unequipped to deal with the great intellectual problems of the times. She was inwardly struggling hard in this way over her scholarly existence and wrestling with the meaning of her life's work.

Under these circumstances she became aware of some things that go back to the time of her youth and which she now began to understand in an entirely new way. Her closest friends at that time had told her that she overestimated her potential, had a naive self-confidence, and did not sufficiently recognize her limits. She now took up this question as her own. And she was victorious over this test of her courage, seeing criticism as a chance to confirm her own lack of knowledge and preparation and to acknowledge what was possible for her to do: to present suggestions and provide an impetus for others to work them out further.

Edith Stein vividly felt the painfulness of this situation and yet found this to be a truly blessed time. She was completely certain inwardly "that it is necessary to go forward step by step and that I may calmly continue to allow providence to guide me."

Edith Stein could lecture at the German Institute for Scientific Pedagogy for only two semesters. The Nazi "seizure of power" put a premature end to her lecturing work. "I have always had affectionate and thankful memories of the beautiful old city and all of the Münster area," she writes later. "Less than one and a half years ago I had come to Münster as a stranger. Now I left behind a large circle of people who were dear and loyal friends." On July 15, 1933, Edith left for Cologne. Friends brought her bouquets of roses to the railroad station, which she took with her to the Carmelite chapel.

Münster i/W. 9. 6. 33.

Ehrwürdige Mater Oberin!

Es hat Fräulein Dr. Edith Stein am Karmel-Kloster angeklopft. Die Vorsehung Gottes, die ihren Weg geebnet hat, führte sie nun auch dorthin.

Sie ist eine begnadete Seele, reich an Gottes- und Menschenliebe, erfüllt mit dem Geiste der Hl. Schrift und der Liturgie, aus der sie schöpft, betet, betrachtet, lebt.

Zwar hat sie durch Wort und Feder, besonders im "Kathol. Akademiker Verband" und im Kathol. Frauenbund," Vieles geleistet. Aber auf solches äussere Wirken möchte sie verzichten, um im Karmel ⟨die eine Perle⟩ Jesus Christus nach dem Vorbild der Hl. Theresia zu finden.

Als Priester und Seelenführer kann ich Ihrem Convent und Ihrem Wohlwollen diese edle, treue Seele nur aufs angelegentlichste empfehlen. Sie wird Allen ein Vorbild tiefster Frömmigkeit und Gebetseifers, — eine Gemeinschaftsfreude voll Güte und Nächstenliebe sein, und still wie ein Strahl Gottes unter Ihnen wandeln.

Gott zum Gruss!
Dr. A. Donders,
Dompropst.

Professor Adolf Donders (born 1877 in Anbolt, died 1944 in Münster), student chaplain, an ardent promoter of the Catholic women's movement, gave Edith Stein a testimonial for her entry into Carmel when she left Münster. Edith also remained in contact with other professors in Münster. In the convent, she felt deeply the suffering of Professor Peter Wust. She maintained a cordial relationship with Professor Bernhard Rosenmöller. When he was transferred to Breslau in 1937, in spite of great danger he took care of Edith's relatives who were still there. A friendship of many years also bound Edith with Professor Baldwin Schwarz (now in Salzburg) and his wife. The last two professors named were later chief witnesses in regard to Edith's attitude toward Judaism and Nazism before her entrance into the Order.

COLOGNE
"To stand before God for all"

The beginning of the year 1933 brought a change in the life of many people, including Edith Stein. The anti-Semitic machinations of the Third Reich put an end to her work as an instructor in Münster. This intrusion into her life did not surprise her. Edith Stein, who from her youth had been a politically keen observer seeing clearly the broad relationships between public and intellectual life, immediately realized that National Socialism not only was a political party, but also professed to be a mythos, a worldview. She set herself a task. In a letter to Pope Pius XI, she argued that marked hostility to Jews is a harbinger of great persecution of Christians and the church. We know how very right she was. She did not receive an answer from Rome.

For many years Edith Stein was absorbed with St. Teresa of Avila, whose heart finally knew nothing more than God and the people whom she wanted to win over to God's service. Eventually, Edith reached the conclusion that the hour had come when she herself had to decide to follow Teresa's path.

Edith Stein did not make this decision lightly. Might it not represent flight from the approaching persecution? However, she believed and knew that it is the Lord himself who was suffering in her Jewish brothers and sisters. Certainly all did not know this. But Edith Stein wanted to stand in for everyone; she wanted to bind herself very closely to the Lord for everyone in order to enter with them into his suffering, which brings redemption for all. She realized beyond a doubt that this was the path laid out for her and that she must follow it in Carmel. She rejected offers that she began to receive to teach abroad. After a difficult leave-taking from her aged mother, Edith Stein entered the Carmel in Cologne on October 14, 1933.

Her life in the Order began quietly. On April 15, 1934, she was accepted as a novice and took the name she herself selected, Teresia Benedicta a Cruce (of the Cross). She joyfully led the daily life of the convent and was even permitted to pursue her intellectual work.

It is often asked what moved Edith Stein, who was, of course, familiar with Benedictine and Dominican spirituality, to decide for the Carmelites. Aside from her relationship to

Teresa of Avila, she was surely attracted by the origin of the Order in the land of her ancestors, and particularly by the tradition of the prophet of Carmel, Elijah, whom the Order calls its father and model. Elijah's saying, "As the Lord lives, before whose face I stand" (1 Kgs 18:15), which is the motto of the friars and nuns of Carmel, must have meant a great deal to Edith.

The first Carmelites came to Cologne in 1637, built a late Baroque church, St. Maria vom Frieden (St. Mary of Peace), and had to leave the property in 1802. Thirty years later Carmelites started a new foundation in Cologne, this time close to the romanesque basilica St. Gereon. They remained there until Bismarck came to power in 1875. In 1899 the Cologne Carmel was activated for a third time. A monastery was built in Cologne-Lindenthal on Dürener Street. This is where Edith entered the Order.

A souvenir card with Edith Stein's handwriting.

Above left: *As was the custom, for the festival High Mass the postulant Edith Stein wore a wedding dress whose white silk was later reworked into a vestment. This was also customary at that time.*

This photo shows the veiling that was customary during Mass at that time. Later Edith wrote about the celebration, "No description can depict how beautiful it was. We continue to receive thank-you letters from guests on whom it also made a very deep impression."

Edith Stein's acceptance ceremony as a novice took place
in the chapel of the Carmel in Cologne-Lindenthal on
April 15, 1934. With her nun's habit she received the
name of Sr. Teresa Benedicta of the Cross, which she
chose for herself. "By the Cross, I understood the fate of
the people of God," she wrote later, "which was then
already beginning to be proclaimed."

The Provincial of the Discalced Carmelites of Germany,
Fr. Theodor Rauch (born 1890 in Alteglofsheim, died
1972 in Regensburg), presided over the clothing
ceremonies. Thanks to his arrangements, the novice was
permitted to resume her intellectual work from then on.

In the nuns' choir of the enclosure Edith Stein recited
the daily office with the other sisters and spent two
hours in silent meditation there. "Whoever enters
Carmel," she writes to a Jewish friend, "is not lost to
her own, but is theirs fully for the first time; it is our
vocation to stand before God for all."

When Edith Stein entered Carmel, Sr. Teresa Renata
Posselt, a distinquished woman, was the novice mistress.
She become prioress in January 1936 and remained so
for many years. She lived through the destruction of the
Carmel in Cologne-Lindenthal by incendiary and
explosive bombs in October 1944. After World War II,
she began the reconstruction of the monastery at its
previous location and so led the convent back to St.
Mary of Peace. In 1948, Mother Renata published the
biography of Edith Stein which went through many
editions and translations. She died in January 1961.

J. M. J. T.

Im Jahre neunzehnhundertfünfunddreißig den 21. April, morgens zwischen 5 und 6 Uhr, im Kloster zum gnadenreichen Jesukinde zu Köln-Lindenthal, legte ihre zeitliche heilige Profeß ab die Chorschwester Theresia Benedikta a Cruce, Tochter des [verstorbenen] Herrn Kaufmann Siegfried Stein und Frau Auguste geborene Courant aus Breslau. Diözese Breslau. Sie legte ihre heiligen Gelübde ab in die Hände der Priorin Schwester Maria Josepha a SS. Sacr., in Gegenwart der Genossenschaft im Alter von 43 Jahren, mit hoher Genehmigung Seiner Eminenz des hochwürdigsten Herrn Kardinal Dr. Karl Joseph Schulte, Erzbischof von Köln, und mit Erlaubnis unseres hochwürdigen Paters Gulielmus a sancto Alberto, vorgesetzten General unseres Ordens, und des hochwürdigen Pater Theodor a S. Francisco, Provinzial.

Sie erhielt das heilige Ordenskleid am 15. April 1934, und sie legte ihre Gelübde ab mit den Worten:

Ich, Schwester Theresia Benedikta a Cruce, mache meine Profeß der zeitlichen Gelübde für drei Jahre und gelobe Gehorsam, Keuschheit und Armut Gott unserm Herrn, der allerseligsten Jungfrau Maria vom Berge Karmel, dem Generaloberen des Ordens der unbeschuhten Karmeliten und Ihnen, ehrwürdige Mutter Priorin, sowie ihren Nachfolgerinnen, nach der ursprünglichen Regel des genannten Ordens und unseren Satzungen.

Vota mea Domino reddam in conspectu omnis populi ejus, in atriis domus Domini.

Schwester Teresia Benedicta a Cruce
Schwester M. Josepha a SS. Sacr. Priorin
Schw. Teresia Renata de Spir. Sto. I. Clav.
Schw. Maria Theresia II Clavarin
Schw. M. Franziska III. Clavarin

At the conclusion of her novitiate years, Edith Stein, Sr. Teresa Benedicta of the Cross, took her first vows on April 21, 1935, which bound her to the Cologne Carmel for three years. The photo shows the entry into the records of the monastery. Beneath the text can also be recognized the signature of Edith Stein: Sr. Teresia Benedicta a Cruce.

KÖLN-HOHENLIND, den   16. Juli 1938

Taufschein.

Rosa Maria Agnes Adelheid S t e i n , geb. am 13. De=
zember 1883, wurde am 24. Dezember 1936 in der St. Elisa=
bethkirche zu Köln-Hohenlind durch Prälat van A c k e n
getauft.

Als Patin war zugegen Berta V e r y in Stellvertre=
tung von Agnes V e r y .

The following year Edith Stein very joyfully witnessed the conversion of her sister Rosa to the Catholic Church. Rosa was baptized in the chapel of St. Elizabeth's Hospital in Cologne-Lindenthal. At that time Edith Stein was a patient in the surgical ward of this clinic because of an accident on the steps in which she broke her wrist and a foot; thus she could be present at the baptismal ceremony. The newly baptized woman received her first holy communion in the chapel of the Carmel on Christmas Eve, 1936.

Edith Stein once wrote from the convent that she was not homesick for Beuron; this subsided when one is in one's true home. What made Carmel home for her? It was the prayer of the church, now no longer in the form of high liturgy, but as silent dialogue of the heart with God. Carmel sets aside two hours a day for meditation, a heritage from Teresa. "What could the prayer of the church be," writes Edith, "if not great lovers giving themselves to God who is love?"

On April 21, 1938, Sister Benedicta took her perpetual vows. But first an incident occurred. It was shortly before the plebiscite of April 10. Everyone knew that there was no longer a strictly secret ballot, that voting "no" could have dire consequences, that the election results were probably rigged anyway. The remark was made among the sisters that it was immaterial how one voted. This utterance disconcerted Edith Stein. With passionate intensity, which no one in the convent had seen in her up to now, she made clear that a system hostile to Christ is to be refused any consent come what may.

There came the government's "Night of Broken Glass," *Kristallnacht,* and with it the greatest danger for anyone who associated with Jews. Therefore, Edith requested a transfer. Surprisingly quickly, the necessary papers for her departure arrived. The house physician of the Carmelites, Dr. Paul Strerath, gladly offered to take the endangered nun across the border in his car. On December 31, 1938, Edith took leave of the Carmel in Cologne.

On the day on which she took her vows, the newly professed nun wore a crown of white roses, as was generally the custom. The photo was taken in the convent garden of the Carmel in Cologne-Lindenthal.

Ich, Schwester Teresia Benedicta a Cruce, mache meine Profeß der einfachen, ewigen Gelübde und verspreche Gehorsam, Keuschheit und Armut Gott, unserem Herrn, der allerseligsten Jungfrau Maria vom Berge Karmel, dem Generaloberen des Ordens der Unbeschuhten Karmeliten und Ihnen, ehrwürdige Mutter Priorin, sowie Ihren Nachfolgerinnen, nach der ursprünglichen Regel des genannten Ordens und unsern Satzungen bis zum Tode:

Tota mea Domina reddam, in conspectu omnis populi eius, in atriis domus Domini.

Karmel Köln-Lindental

21. April 1938.

Three years after her first profession, Edith Stein took the perpetual vows of a Carmelite and thereby became a member of the convent with both a passive and an active vote. The photograph shows the profession document in Edith Stein's handwriting. It is customary in Carmel to place this document into the coffins of deceased sisters. Edith Stein's profession document was preserved. Edith understood her perpetual vows not only as binding her to the order of Carmel, but as a promise to surrender her life irrevocably. Thus she seizes on the idea of standing in for others as a divine calling. She takes this to be her innermost destiny. It is as if all the external events that would overtake her had only this one point of fulfilling her inner calling. "I am confident," she wrote shortly after her perpetual vows, "that the Lord has accepted my life for everyone. I am reminded repeatedly of Queen Esther who was taken from her people precisely to stand before the king for the people. I am a very poor and powerless Esther, but the King who has chosen me is eternally great and compassionate."

63

Mein einziger Beruf ist fortan nur mehr lieben
(Hl. V Johannes vom Kreuz, Geistlicher Gesang)

ANDENKEN
AN MEINE EWIGE HL. PROFESS
(21. April 1938)

UND MEIN SCHLEIERFEST
(Sonntag vom Guten Hirten, 1. Mai 1938)
im Karmel, Köln=Lindenthal

SCHWESTER TERESIA BENEDICTA
a Cruce, O. C. D.
(Edith Stein)

Souvenir card of Edith Stein's perpetual vows and veiling ceremony. It was usual at that time for the so-called veiling ceremony not to take place until several days after the perpetual vows. At a festive Mass the inductee received the black veil instead of the former white one.

Ewige Gelübde 21. IV.
Alleluja!

E i n l a d u n g

zum Schleierfest einer

Schwester, das Sonntag, den 1. Mai, in der

Klosterkirche der Karmelitinnen, Köln-Lin-

denthal, Dürener Straße 89, gefeiert wird.

9 Uhr Hochamt, anschließend Ansprache, Wei-

he und Ueberreichung des schwarzen Schleiers.

Though the vows were pronounced in complete privacy, the veiling ceremony was a public celebration to which guests were invited. Edith Stein added a handwritten message for her friends to the mimeographed invitation. Suffragan Bishop Dr. Josef Stockums celebrated the High Mass with its festive homily and conducted the ceremony of presenting her with the black veil. Edith had taken her first vows (April 21, 1935) on Easter Sunday morning. This point in time meant a great deal to her. The perpetual vows three years later fell on the Thursday after Easter, and May 1 fell on the second Sunday after Easter, at that time called Good Shepherd Sunday. The clothing ceremony had also fallen on this Sunday (April 15, 1934). She writes to a friend, "I rejoice every day that Easter time is so long and that one can continue to appropriate more and more of its inexhaustible riches. It is really the time of the church year when we are closest to heaven. The blossoming trees and sprouting perennials in our garden are, moreover, inextricably linked with the great days of blessing in my monastery life."

After the violence of the government's Kristallnacht, Edith Stein decided to emigrate to a foreign Carmel. Her plan of going to a monastery in the Holy Land fell through. So she chose Echt in Holland. Edith Stein needed a photo for her passport. This picture was taken on the threshold of the open door of the enclosure. On the whitewashed wall of the convent passage, one can very faintly recognize the cross hanging there that can be seen over the head of Sr. Benedicta of the Cross.

Before Edith Stein left Cologne, Dr. Strerath drove her to St. Mary of Peace, the former Carmelite church, at that time a parish church, in the old section of Cologne. Edith had expressed the wish to pray one last time before the icon of the Queen of Peace. The buildings that dated from the seventeenth century and in which the Carmelites had lived until 1802 were also shown to her. The picture shows the sanctuary before its destruction in 1942. The monastery at Cologne-Lindenthal was also destroyed. After the Second World War, the Carmelites rebuilt the church and monastery of St. Mary of Peace and moved onto their old property in 1949.

ECHT
"For departure ... for the rest of my life"

With her characteristic clarity of vision, Edith Stein suspected that her departure from Cologne was a departure forever. She moved to Echt, a small town in Netherlands. There was a Carmel there founded by Cologne during the time of the Bismarckian *Kulturkampf.* Edith was received with a heartfelt willingness to help her, and she soon felt at home in Echt—hidden in the will of God. So she wrote.

The sisters in Cologne considered neutral Holland as a secure haven. Nevertheless, it was not easy in this country overrun with refugees to obtain approval for permanent residency. It became even more difficult the following year when her sister, Rosa Stein, a Catholic like Edith, followed her to Echt. But things finally worked out, and Rosa was installed as an extern sister at the convent.

The sisters were both filled with gratitude, for being together as well. Yet it was still difficult for both of them. The family had been broken up and scattered throughout the world, and those remaining in Germany threatened with death. When [with the German occupation] the persecution of the Jews also began in the Netherlands, more and more horrifying news penetrated into the convent, which Rosa as extern sister brought from outside.

The Carmelite monastery in Echt/Limburg, Bovenstestraat 48 where Edith Stein was received as a guest on December 31, 1938. At that time the sisters spoke German exclusively. It was only in 1941 when five young ladies entered as novices that they switched to Dutch. In a very short time, Edith completely mastered the language.

Above left: *At times Edith had to take care of the refectory in the monastery. Also she often gladly undertook the readings during mealtimes.*

Above right: *The hallway to the cells at the Carmel in Echt. On the right side can be seen the door to Edith Stein's cell (the fourth door from the front).*

▶

Some time after Edith Stein (from July 1, 1939), her sister Rosa also found a haven at the Carmel in Echt. She took over the work of extern sister of the monastery and helped in the garden. The photo of the two sisters was taken there.

Interior of the cell that Edith Stein occupied in the Carmel in Echt. Here she wrote The Science of the Cross, *her last work.*

Perhaps in order to distract Sr. Benedicta from the constant agitation over the bad news, the superior again gave her scholarly work. For the anniversary of the "Mystical Doctor of the Church and the Father of the Carmelites," St. John of the Cross, Edith was to present his life and his doctrine in a book. She considered her immersion in the work of this saint a particular blessing. She felt that the nets of the persecutors were being pulled ever more tightly around her. Efforts to arrange a flight to Switzerland never got very far. After the Dutch bishops make a public protest against the deportation of Jews, there was a reprisal: On August 2, 1942, Edith and Rosa Stein, along with all Catholic Jews, were deported to the assembly camps in Amersfoort and Westerbork, and then on August 7 to the east. There the trail of the sisters is lost. Results of long investigations thus far show that both were killed on August 9 in Auschwitz-Birkenau.

Ich danke meinen lieben
Vorgesetzten und allen lieben Mit-
schwestern von ganzem Herzen für die
Liebe, mit der sie mich aufgenommen
haben, und für alles Gute, das mir
in diesem Hause zuteil wurde.

Schon jetzt nehme ich den Tod,
den Gott mir zugedacht hat, in vollkommener
Unterwerfung unter Seinen heiligsten Willen
mit Freuden entgegen. Ich bitte den
Herrn, daß Er mein Leben und Sterben an-
nehmen möchte zu Seiner Ehre und Ver-
herrlichung, für alle Anliegen der heiligsten Herzen Jesu und Mariae und der
heiligen Kirche, insbesondere für die Erhaltung,
Heiligung und Vollendung unseres heiligen

Edith Stein wrote a will in the Echt Carmel. It contains proposals for her books and manuscripts. Above all, however, this will is a spiritual testament. These lines are a part of it.

Ordens, namentlich des Kölner und des Echter Karmels, zur Sühne für den Unglauben des jüdischen Volkes und damit der Herr von den Seinen aufgenommen werde und Sein Reich komme in Herrlichkeit, für die Rettung Deutschlands und den Frieden der Welt; schließlich für meine Angehörigen, Lebende und Tote, und alle, die mir Gott gegeben hat: daß keines von ihnen verloren gehe.

Am Freitag in der Fronleichnamsoktav, 9. Juni 1939, dem 7. Tag meiner hl. Exerzitien.

In nomine Patris et Filii et Spiritus Sancti. Sch. Teresia Benedicta a Cruce, O. C. D.

The last photographs of Rosa and Edith Stein,
probably in spring or summer 1942.

72

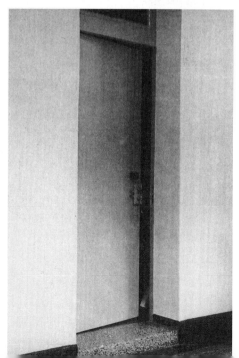

Above: *In the choir of the enclosure, Edith Stein prayed silently on the afternoon of August 2, 1942, as two Gestapo people from the Nazi occupying power gained entrance into the monastery and asked to speak to the sisters.*

Above right: *At the grille of the reception room the two men explained that Edith and Rosa Stein were under arrest and demanded that they accompany them immediately. After useless arguments, during which the prioress requested a postponement because of the ongoing emigration efforts, the two sisters left the house with the Gestapo people.*

The enclosure door in the Carmel in Echt through ▶ *which Edith Stein left the monastery.*

The police car did not wait right at the front door but closer to the street corner. Excited and protesting people had already assembled there. Also, a friend of the Carmel who had been quickly called to the scene was able to get so close to the two arrested women that they could clearly hear Edith's exhortation to her weeping sister Rosa: Come, let us go for our people!"

What meaning did John of the Cross have for Edith Stein during the last months of her life? Doubtless Edith had long known she was bound up with this saint. She often read his works and meditated on his spiritual poetry. And, above all, she chose, like him, the subtitle "of the Cross." In the Discalced Carmelite Order, such titles indicate the vocation and readiness to live out certain mysteries of faith. For John of the Cross and for Edith Stein the cross signified the epitome of the surrender of Jesus to his fate as a human

being, that he—trusting the Father in heaven—lived and suffered on earth in order to bring all people home from sin and damnation into the house of the Father, which has many rooms and a place for all.

There are many indications that Edith Stein found her true self in John of the Cross. Here only a few examples can be mentioned. For instance, she spoke of the calling and selection of certain persons that removes them from association with others and makes them a sign of contradiction, because the Most

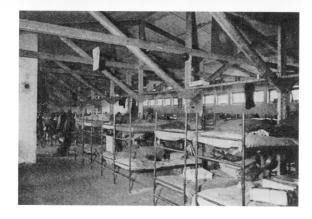

The police car took the arrested women first to an intermediate station in Amersfoort and then to the assembly camp of Westerbork. There the transport containing only Jews who had been baptized as Catholics arrived on August 4. Among those imprisoned were a remarkably large number of religious. At the camp the prisoners realized that the whole thing was a retribution for the public stance of the bishops against the deportation of Jews. One of the prisoners wrote from Westerbork, "I go with courage and trust and joy—as do the nuns who are with me. We are permitted to witness for Jesus and with our bishops to witness for the truth...."

At the Carmelite monastery of La Pâquier in Switzerland, the cell that Edith was to occupy was already prepared. But all the rescue attempts came too late.

High has laid a hand on them. Also, she reflected on the image of the Messiah who courts his bride, Israel, and by doing so does not avoid death on the cross in order to attain life for her. For God's plans for salvation do indeed pertain to God's chosen people but, as Edith Stein knew, are also for the sake of all humanity.

In her fragmentary last work, *The Science of the Cross*, Edith Stein tried to interpret what she, after long efforts, had been able to comprehend about the essence of human life. Thus, in the end, her youthful life-plan of "serving humanity" with her gifts and efforts and the laying down of her life with Christ "for the sake of humanity" converge into a great meaningful whole.

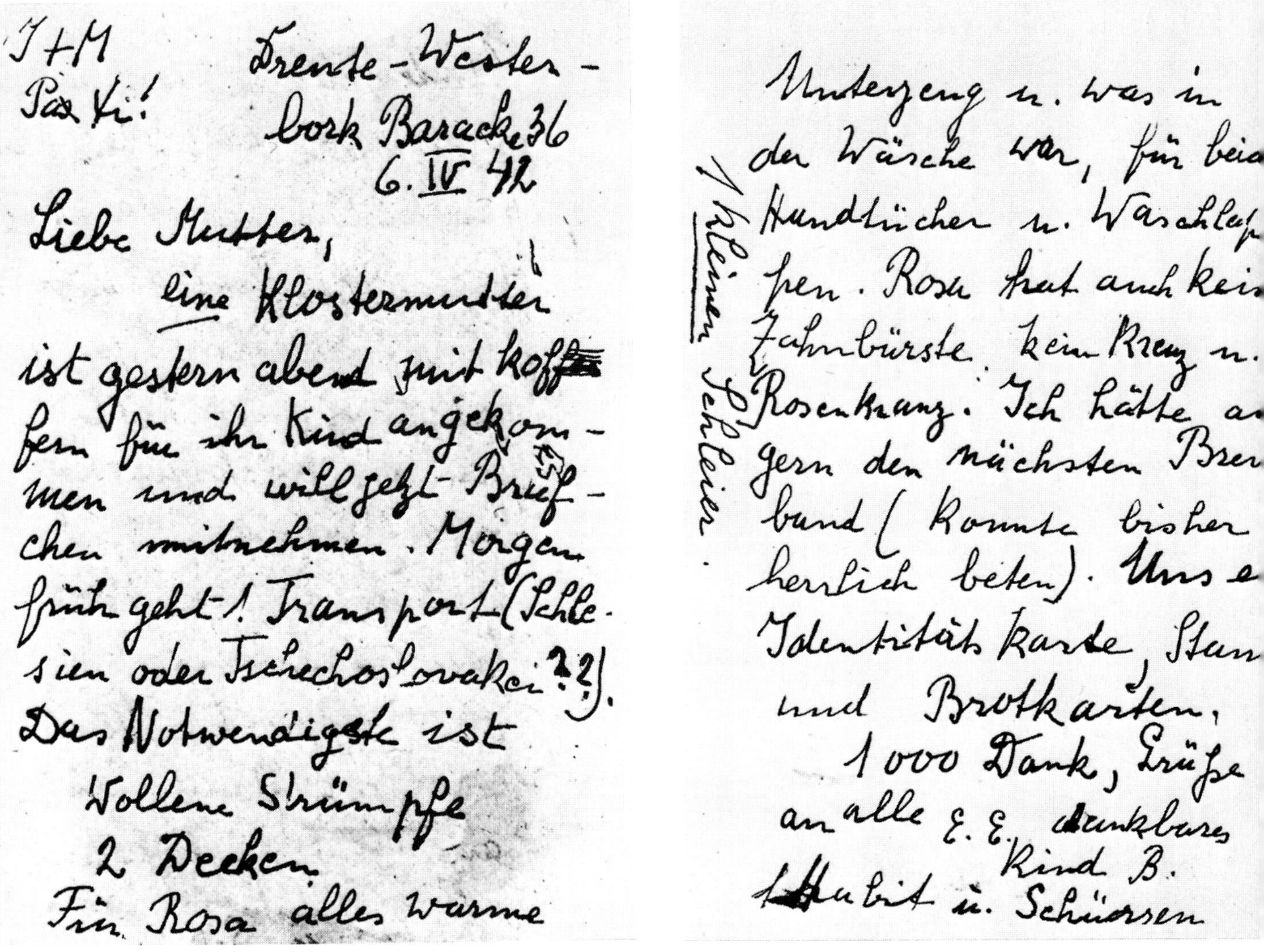

J+M
Pax Ki!

Trente-Wester-
bork Baracke 36
6. IV 42

Liebe Mutter,

eine Klostermutter ist gestern abend mit koffern für ihr Kind angekommen und will jetzt Briefchen mitnehmen. Morgen früh geht 1. Transport (Schlesien oder Tschechoslovakei??). Das Notwendigste ist

Wollene Strümpfe
2 Decken
Für Rosa alles Warme

/kleinen Schleier.

Unterzeug u. was in der Wäsche war, für beide Handtücher u. Waschlappen. Rosa hat auch keine Zahnbürste, kein Kreuz u. Rosenkranz. Ich hätte auch gern den nächsten Breviband (konnte bisher herrlich beten). Uns e... Identitätskarte, Stam... und Brotkarten.

1000 Dank, Grüße an alle E.E. dankbares Kind B.
Habit u. Schürzen

Karmelitinnen -
Kloster Echt
        Bovenstestraat 48
Schw. Teresia Benedicta
a Cruce (Edith Stein)
    Rosa Stein,
Schweizer Konsulat
Amsterdam C
Herengracht 545,
möge sorgen, daß
wir möglichst bald
über die Grenze

kommen, Für Reise-
geld wird unser
Kloster sorgen.

Page 76: *In Westerbork the prisoners were still permitted to send out letters and also receive visitors, who could bring them clothing, bedding, or medicine. The Carmel in Echt had even sent to the Stein sisters two young men, who brought them suitcases and took back from Sr. Benedicta to the prioress of the Carmel a note hastily scribbled on calendar pages. Edith made an error in the date: It was August, 6, 1942. A number of other nuns were imprisoned in the camp along with Edith. The first sentence refers to the visit that one of these sisters had from her superior.*

◀

Edith Stein probably made these notes for the sisters in Echt to ask them at the last minute to make one last effort at the Swiss Consulate for permission to emigrate.

In the early morning of August 7th, the transport left Westerbork. First the train traveled south and passed the station in Schifferstadt in the Palatinate, where it stopped for a rather long time. Here Edith Stein must have found the opportunity to give short reports to acquaintances. In any case, a number of witnesses have stated that a woman dressed in dark clothing, who called herself Edith Stein, gave them a short message orally or even in writing: "We are on the road to the east!"

◄

A certificate from the Dutch Red Cross regarding the death of Edith Stein. In the Dutch official gazette of February 16, 1950, the Ministry of Justice had given the date of death as August 9 as the most likely date according to the information available. Rosa Stein died in Auschwitz-Birkenau on the same day. The victims of this transport were not delivered to the work camp before being killed in the gas chambers. Therefore, their names do not appear on the prisoner lists of Auschwitz. The document states that the transport of Catholic Jews that left Westerbork on August 7 arrived in Auschwitz on August 9.

Kreuzzeichnung des hl. Johannes vom Kreuz [1542 - 1591; Original in Ávila, Convento de la Encarmación].

Edith Stein worked for more than a year at the end of her earthly life on her last work, The Science of the Cross. *While doing so, she often looked at a small image of the Crucified which St. John of the Cross had once drawn. It was an inadequate reproduction on inferior paper. Therefore, Sr. Benedicta of the Cross tried to draw it and wrote about her efforts, "I am not an artist at all, but I did it with reverence and love."*

CITATION REFERENCES

Whenever possible, quotations have been taken from existing English translations of Edith Stein's works, with minor changes in wording as needed.

BRESLAU

"We are in the world…" (*Life in a Jewish Family,* trans. Josephine Koeppel [Washington, DC: ICS Publications, 1986]: 177).

"I, Edith Stein, was born…" (Biography in her dissertation, *On the Problem of Empathy,* trans. Waltraut Stein, 3d rev. ed. [Washington, DC: ICS Publications, 1989]: 119).

"I was fed up with learning" (*Life,* 145).

"deliberately and consciously…" (*Life,* 148).

"constant exertion of all my powers…" (see *Life,* 215).

"So I lived in the naive self-delusion…" and "…often in a mocking and ironic tone" (see *Life,* 195-196).

GÖTTINGEN

"Glimpse into new worlds" (see *Life,* 249).

"almost without noticing it, gradually transformed" (*Life,* 261).

"Here I would have been able…" (*Life,* 217).

"The attention is turned away…" (see *Life,* 250).

"lacked the necessary foundation" and "consisted precisely of such work of clarification and one forged the conceptual framework for oneself" (see *Life,* 222).

"… the most important decision of my life" (see *Life,* 239).

"hitherto totally unknown world" (*Life,* 260).

"more depth and beauty…" (*Life,* 308).

"the beginning of a new phase of my life" (*Life,* 268).

FREIBURG

"to obey is something I cannot do" (*Self-Portrait in Letters, 1916-1942,* trans. Josephine Koeppel [Washington, DC: ICS Publications, 1993]: 22; letter to Roman Ingarden, 2/19/1918).

"Are you by chance also among them?" (see *Life,* 399).

"Strictly ABC instruction" (*Letters,* 17; letter to Roman Ingarden, 5/31/1917).

"Pray for me…" (*Letters,* 12; letter to Roman Ingarden, 3/17/1917).

"always remain the master…" (*Letters,* 37–38; letter to Fritz Kaufmann, 11/22/1918).

BERGZABERN

"That's my secret" (from the memoirs of Hedwig Conrad-Martius ["secretum meum mihi"], cited in *Hochland* 51 [October 1958]: 38).

"…on tenterhooks" to "human support" (see *Life,* 235–237).

"In the summer of 1921…" (from Edith Stein's sketch, "How I Came to the Cologne Carmel," in *Edith Stein: Selected Writings,* trans. Susanne M. Batzdorff [Springfield, IL: Templegate Publishers, 1990]: 19).

SPEYER

"I have a small, simple truth to express" (See *Letters,* 87; letter to Adelgundis Jaegerschmid, 4/28/1931).

"I am only an instrument…" (see *Letters,* 77; letter to Erna Hermann, 12/19/1930).

"difficult and much debated question…" (*Essays on Woman,* trans. Freda Mary Oben, 2d ed. [Washington, DC: ICS Publications, 1996]: 83).

"In terms of dogma…" (see *Woman,* 84).

"Whether ordained or not ordained…" (see *Woman,* 84).

"Only the most purely developed…" (see *Woman,* 56).

BEURON

"Like the vestibule of heaven" (see *Edith Stein: Selected Writings,* 21).

MÜNSTER

"where my limits lie" (*Letters,* 125; letter to Hedwig Conrad-Martius, 11/13/1932).

"that things are as they should be" (*Letters,* 94; letter to Adelgundis Jaegerschmid, 6/28/1931).

"…who are totally caught up…" (*Letters,* 126; letter to Hedwig Conrad-Martius, 11/13/1932).

"that it is necessary…" (*Letters,* 139; letter to Hedwig Conrad-Martius, 4/5/1933).

COLOGNE

"to stand before God for all" (*Letters,* 178; letter to Fritz Kaufmann, 5/14/1934).

"What could the prayer of the church be…" (from "The Prayer of the Church," in *The Hidden Life,* trans. Waltraut Stein [Washington, DC: ICS Publications, 1992]: 15).

ECHT

"for departure…for the rest of my life" (*Letters,* 300; letter to Annie Greven, 1/14/1939).

EDITH STEINS WERKE, edited by Lucy Gelber, Romäus Leuven, O.C.D., and Michael Linssen, O.C.D.

Band I: *Kreuzeswissenschaft. Studie über Johannes a Cruce.* Druten: De Maas & Waler; Freiburg: Herder, 1983.
[**Science of the Cross. Trans. Josephine Koeppel. Washington, DC: ICS Publications, 1999.**]

Band II: *Endliches und ewiges Sein. Versuch eines Aufstiegs zum Sinn des Seins.* Freiburg: Herder, 1986.
[**Finite and Eternal Being. An Attempt to Ascend to the Meaning of Being. Trans. Kurt F. Reinhardt. Washington, DC: ICS Publications, 1999.**]

Band V: *Die Frau. Ihre Aufgabe nach Natur und Gnade.* Louvain: Nauwelaerts; Freiburg: Herder, 1959.
[**Essays on Woman. Trans. Freda Mary Oben. 2d ed. Washington, DC: ICS Publications, 1996.**]

Band VI: *Welt und Person. Ein Beitrag zum christlichen Wahrheitsstreben* (World and Person. A Contribution to the Christian Search for Truth). Louvain: Nauwelaerts; Freiburg: Herder, 1962.

Band VII: *Aus dem Leben einer jüdischen Familie. Das Leben Edith Steins: Kindheit und Jugend.* Complete ed. Druten: De Maas & Waler; Herder: Freiburg, 1985.
[**Life in a Jewish Family, 1891-1916. Trans. Josephine Koeppel. Washington, DC: ICS Publications, 1986.**]

Band VIII and IX: *Selbstbildnis in Briefen. Erster Teil 1916–1934. Zweiter Teil 1934–1942.* Druten: De Maas & Walter; Freiburg: Herder, 1976.
[**Self Portrait in Letters, 1916–1942. Trans. Josephine Koeppel. Washington, DC: ICS Publications, 1993.**]

Band X: Romäus Leuven. *Heil im Unheil. Das Leben Edith Steins: Reife und Vollendung* (Sanity in Madness. The life of Edith Stein: Maturity and Consummation). Druten: De Maas & Walter; Freiburg: Herder, 1983.

Band XI: *Verborgenes Leben: Hagiographische Essays, Meditationen, Geistliche Texte.* Druten: De Maas & Walter; Freiburg: Herder, 1987.
[**The Hidden Life: Hagiographic Essays, Meditations, Spiritual Texts. Trans. Waltraut Stein. Washington, DC: ICS Publications, 1992.**]

OTHER WORKS

Edith Stein, eine grosse Frau unseres Jahrhunderts. Ein Lebensbild, gewonnen aus Erinnerungen und Briefen durch Sr. Teresia Renata de Spiritu Sancto, O.C.D. (Posselt). Nürnberg: Glock and Lutz, 1954.
[Sister Teresia de Spiritu Sancto, O.D.C. *Edith Stein.* Trans. Cecily Hastings and Donald Nicholl. New York: Sheed and Ward, 1952.]

Kleines Philosophisches Wörterbuch (Little Philosophical Dictionary). Freiburg: Herder-Bücherei, No. 16, 1958.

Stein, Edith. *On the Problem of Empathy.* Trans. Waltraut Stein. 3d rev. ed. Washington, DC: ICS Publications, 1989. (This is Edith Stein's doctoral dissertation done under Husserl.)

NOTE: The volumes of the Collected Works of Edith Stein available from ICS Publications are indicated above in bold.

Chronology of Events and Dates in the Life of Edith Stein

1891	*October 12:* Born as a Jew in Breslau.
1911	High school diploma with honors.
1911–1913	Studies in Breslau: German, history, psychology, and philosophy.
1913–1915	Studies in Göttingen: philosophy (Husserl), German, history.
1915	*Staatsexamen* (course exam) in Göttingen with honors.
	Service in a typhoid military hospital for the Red Cross in Mährisch-Weisskirchen.
1916	Assistant instructor in Breslau.
	Doctoral exam in Freiburg, *summa cum laude.*
1916–1918	Research assistant to Edmund Husserl in Freiburg.
1919–1923	Private scholarly work; fruitless attempts to qualify as a university lecturer.
1921	Reading of the *Life* of St. Teresa of Avila in the Conrad-Martius house in Bergzabern/Pfalz; conversion decision.
1922	*January 1:* Baptism and first Holy Communion in the parish church of St. Martin in Bergzabern.
	February 2: Confirmation in the private chapel of the bishop of Speyer.
1923–1931	Teacher at St. Magdalene's, the Dominican girls' school and education school in Speyer.
	Translation work and other literary work.
	Domestic and foreign lecture tours.
1932–1933	Instructor at the German Institute for Scientific Pedagogy in Münster.
1933	*October 14:* Entrance into the Carmel in Cologne.
1934	*April 15:* Clothing as Sister Teresia Benedicta a Cruce.
1935	*April 21:* Taking of First Vows. Profession for three years.
1938	*April 21:* Perpetual vows.
	May 1: So-called veiling celebration.
	December 31: Emigration to Echt, Holland.
1934–1942	Production of her most important works, *Finite and Eternal Being* and *Science of the Cross,* and also many shorter works.

1942	*August 2:* Arrest and transport to Amersfoort.
	August 4: Continuation from Amersfoort to Camp Westerbork.
	August 9: Arrival in Auschwitz, murder in Birkenau.
1962	*January 4:* Initiation of the ecclesiastical process for the beatification of Edith Stein by the Archbishop of Cologne, Cardinal Josef Frings.
	July 25: Initiation of the examination of the writings of Edith Stein.
1971	*July 7:* Celebration of the conclusion of the examination of writings in Cologne.
	March 7: Initiation of the third part of the process: "De-non-cultu."
1972	*August 9:* Conclusion of the entire diocesan process by Cardinal Höffner in a celebration at the Cologne Carmel of the thirtieth anniversary of Edith Stein's death; in conjunction with this, the transfer of all the documents to Rome.
1987	*May 1:* Beatification of Edith Stein by Pope John Paul II in Cologne.
1998	*October 11:* Canonization by Pope John Paul II at St. Peter's in Rome.

The Institute of Carmelite Studies promotes research and publication in the field of Carmelite spirituality. Its members are Discalced Carmelites, part of a Roman Catholic community—friars, nuns, and laity—who are heirs to the teaching and way of life of Teresa of Jesus and John of the Cross, men and women dedicated to contemplation and to ministry in the church and the world. Information concerning their way of life is available through local diocesan Vocation Offices, or from the Vocation Director's Office, 1525 Carmel Road, Hubertus, WI, 53033.